Barking Geckos
Stories and Observations in Poetic Prose

by Branch Isole

For Carol –
All the Best
Branch Isole

Barking Geckos
Stories and Observations in Poetic Prose
by Branch Isole

Printed in the United States of America

Library of Congress Control Number: 2004101141
ISBN 0-9747692-2-3

Mana'o Publishing
PO Box 1696
Lahaina, HI 96767

Barking Geckos contains adult material and language some of which is sexually explicit in nature. It is intended for mature audiences only.

Contents

Introduction

In the Hawaiian culture, Geckos are bearers of good luck.

If you have ever visited Hawaii, you may have heard a Gecko "bark." This is the distinctive sound Geckos make at night when they want to get your attention. Not knowing where this audible noise comes from the first time you encounter it, can be startling. You glance around the room or lanai (patio) and soon realize that the only thing there, other than you, is a three inch lizard on the wall or ceiling, waiting patiently to tell you a story.

These small reptilians are the descendants of thousands of years of evolution. Keep your eyes on this amazing creature and you will see a world of struggle, beauty and survival unfold. They have much to reveal about life and the process of existence.

So the next time you are in Hawaii, relax and listen . . . perhaps the *Barking Geckos* are about to share with you, one of their stories.

Branch Isole

I've got something inside me
but it's not what my life's about
cause I've been letting my outside tide me
over 'til my time runs out.

50 Years

50 years have come and gone
50 years of feeling strong
50 years of being alone
50 years preparing for home
50 years I thought I knew
50 years of red, white and blue
50 years deceived and lied to
50 years I never knew

One year lived by reason and rhyme
One year lived . . . . 50 times.

Anniversary

From Paper and Cotton
to Silver and Gold
Our story together
still unfolds
Each year's magnificence
remembered by significance
A gift to mark
each passing milestone
A love shared together
Love, we might not have known

We said our vows
It seems a lifetime ago,
Where the time goes
No one really knows

We acknowledge yet
another year,
One more anniversary

Remembering that wonderful day
when you and I,
became We.

Barbie

Sweeping, swirling,
gliding on the wing
Thoughts of you
allow my heart to sing
of ages past
present days
futures unknown
Once again, forever alone

One note at a time
struggling to find
just the right
conjunctive rhyme
Blended slowly
from bass and treble
Crescendo building
You,
an unruly rebel

A hungered groupie
caught naked on tour
Enjoying self indulgence
just once more
Reaching the door
and playing the whore

White knight slaying all
who might steal your amour

Perfection please;
Scalpel
piece by piece,
trim, nip and tuck
Silicone
Cellulite
Collagen
when is it ever enough?
Once, no twice, no wait
yet thrice,
then four,
then…
even more

The house
Picket fence
The cat and the dog
A self-centerted mist
Swallowing all who venture
To peer through its fog

Of thought of word of deed
where to look
To find a seed,
one to fulfill
that burning need,

a need of something
greater than greed

Poor and alone
again this to know,
Your thought,
it was always
win
place
or show
Now, where to turn
which way to go?
Where's the shining man
come to claim his own?

What were your dreams
and where did they lead?
Are you still dreaming today
or did they each slip
slowly away?

What does it take
for you to see
Nothing more than you
and your spirit
for me.

Beautiful People

There are so many
beautiful people
in the world today

On some it shows
in others it grows
A truer understanding
of beauty however
is evidently exposed
and most oft found
when open mouths
do expound

Wordsmiths nay
may they be
but he or she
who communicates effectively,
Always, head and shoulders above others
will they be

So teach your children
that cosmetic beauty
is only surface, skin deep
While for the well read and balanced
rewards and blessings
will they reap.

Best Friend

My lungs are blacker
than a coal mine shaft
but I'm not quite convinced
it's from smokin' three packs a day
or my two pouches
of chewing tobaccer

Yes it's true that my liver's shot
but it's not because I drink a lot
How much is too much
beyond medicinal?
The fifth's I need are truly visceral

More a lover
than a fighter
My temper has, one igniter
Do or say
things that offend
I'll break you so you never bend
again

Money?
I'm a little in debt
Got some bills
I haven't paid yet
Know my way around a tort

Been three or four times
to bankruptcy court

Lived with the same woman
going on twenty-two years
We've had some laughs
some hard times
some tears
She must love me
that's for sure
she keeps coming back
for more and more

I always like
to treat her right,
even when it comes
to our fist fights
She's filed charges
of assault,
but it's never once
been my fault

Yea,
she's left me a couple of times
no matter the reason
no matter the rhyme

Somehow,
we always get back together
I beg,
she concedes
I blame the weather

We've been divorced
and remarried
three separate times
Now I ask, is that a crime?

I always do my j-o-b
even if my boss is an SOB
He says, "you're not punctual enough"
I tell him what to shove

So I've been late
every once in a while
He doesn't need to
treat me like a child
Besides, I've always got
a great excuse
I'm cool,
I like to stay loose

Now, I know
I'm not always right
in fact I made a mistake once,
it was a Tuesday night

I'll never forget it
for as long as I live
I had to protect myself
and use my shiv

So I murdered
that lying scum bag
He deserved
to have his toe tagged

The world is against me
most of the time
and I have to defend
and protect me and mine

They say my behavior
is reckless abandon
I say, 'Sorry'
I'd like to make amends
but Denial,
is my best friend.

Between

Between
entering, and leaving alone
Between
coming, and going home
Between
birth, and death atoned
Each life is spent searching
attempting to be a part
of something
of anything
of everything
Except,
Apart

Lifeline severed
mind, body and soul
separated
Free to discover
who we are,
Not

We look outward
for recognition from others
to know
who we are,
Not

So we will not have to look inward
to know and recognize
who we are,
Not

All
we think
and believe
Is couched in what
we think
and believe
Others will think
and believe
About who we are,
Not

We arrive as aliens
in this strange reality,
this foreign place
and time,
Travelers

Trying to discover
Trying to find
Who we are,
Not

We come
with a knowledge
of the cosmic universe
and all its secrets held,
Within

Buried deep
under layer upon layer
of blood, flesh and skin
Masked behind
and veiled beneath
all earthly matters,
Is Us

Between
first and last breath.

Café Queen

Betwixt tank tops
and sables
she weaves
she winds
around chairs
and tables

Queen
of the meal time jungle
feeding her tribe
serving their needs
from dawn to dusk
midst the praise and the fuss

She sees them come
She sees them go
Here, a piece of pie
There, a cup of joe

On her feet
hour upon hour
no time for a break,
minimum wage
and tips to be made

Serving a mass to singles,
and singular masses
Cleaning up spills
and assessing,
gastric gases

Reuben for the professor
from the U's ivory tower
Baked Alaska and milk
for the postman
who's come in from the shower
and a low carb Cobb salad
for the proprietor of flowers

Slinging hash
Trading cash
Taking out
the kitchen trash

An unsung heroine
of daily commerce
'Grand Dame'
of the short order matrix
The hard working ladies
of cafés and diners,
The American waitress.

-for Donna

Choices

The game or the gift
The lust or the love
The darkness or light
The loss, or blessing from above.

You approach with your thoughts.

War and peace
Aloneness and pleasing
Poverty and pleasure
Listening to them and hearing you,

You allow us to know our deeds.

Poetry, prose
Parable lessons
The words flow in statements
from each learning session.

You teach us by your word.

Your guarantee; our release.

Cruel and Usual

Of all God's creatures
large and small
the cruelest by far
of them all
is the human child
at about age ten,
That is
of course
until he grows
to be a man
Then he can become
a true abuser,
a tyrant
and demonizer
of his own
children and women
and start the cycle
all over again

When the Bible instructs
as to seven generations
of admonishing woes,
it's not always
of plagues
and perils
and pain,

but of inappropriate
hateful
and unloving behavior
that flows,
from parent to child
and to subsequent offspring,
and so it goes
and so it goes

If you want to identify
this behavior for yourself
just look around
and you will see
the fruit doesn't fall
far from the tree

Once a child learns
what he or she sees
and experiences
first hand,
be it open or fist
or a twist of the wrist
out of anger
and anguish
of insecurity,
the pattern is set
into perpetuity

So if you observe it
ask someone involved
to be the adult
and put a stop to it all,
immediately

And if it is your own behavior
towards the ones
you so called 'love'
then seek aid
and assistance
from both here
and above

Break the cycle
of abuse
once and for all!
That both you
and your children
may again,
stand tall.

Dandelion

Love's me,
Love's me not

Love with conditions
is about control.

Day Dream Visions

blue skies, white clouds
both up above
wisps of vapor trails mix
becoming figments of imagination
born on high
coming to life
before my very eyes
a rabbit here and there a dragon
and what is this?
a clown doing tricks.

Diver Down

Time to prepare
for the evening meal
What shall we have?
For what do you feel?

Meat or fish
Thai, French or Mexican
Perhaps,
a vegetarian dish
What is your wish?

We could opt for a salad
before our main entrée
or more simple yet,
dipped bread and butter
in the house vinaigrette

In this land of plenty
and over abundance
we always eat everywhere
at least more than once

The key to acquiring
the kitchen's best
is to be first in line
ahead of the rest

Sittings and settings
never a problem pose
for we bring our own
digit utensils
and have no chair needs
in which to repose

We are the homeless
in this Home of the Brave
The 'Haves'
ignore us
and label us naives
but as long as you wasters
keep on thriving
we dinner dumpster divers
will keep on diving.

Electrical Orchestration

Remove from me all matter Lord
all gas and liquid too
Leave only the electric charge
that was me originally, from You.

Take the soul and spirit aura
of these molecules
which were of and by,
and with You before

Since the beginning
when they were combined
in new form
from the myriad of possibilities
of all your worlds

Reconstitute them once more Lord
in a fashion of your choice
That the new me
might be, more like You

That the new charge
re-formed from your hands
this time,
might serve You
instead of myself.

End Times

Eight of ten horns
Now in place
Two more to go
Time to pick up the pace

Two formal states
now only debate
Their history filled
with suspicion and hate

'Roadmap to Peace'
Anti-Emmanuel soon released
Awaiting his invitations
amends to make
on his path of intentions

Armies assembled
both east and west
Caustic spark?
anyone's guess

Come to aid, to the rescue
To lead, to stand in the gap
Reconciler for the Jew
Leader of the trap

Patiently waiting
groomed for lies and deceit
In the wings
preparations for worldly feats
One like us
master of earthly tricks
His nemesis' sign;
six six six.

Enemy of the State

Sitting shock still
two movements only
ever take place
without her will

Lungs inflate briefly
exchanging gases
at the speed of
cold flowing molasses

A slow shallow breath
indiscernibly escapes
as if her last
just before death

Sole other involuntary response
her body makes,
pupil size adjusting
to light intake

Neither of these
will ever disclose
their host's location,
no matter where she be
no matter her station

Invisibility is her key
to long lasting
job security

This is her assignment
This is her task
To do what is told
and never to ask

Blending in
with her environs
a killer lurks
and waits
For exactly the right
moment of impact
to take place

Clothing and skin match perfectly
whatever her background cover
Be she disguised as the sea
or venerable landlubber

So real her camouflage
even she glances twice
to see if the graphic
is printed, .
or real mice

Details so real
tricking the mind's eye
of both casual observer
and astute connoisseur

Third step of the process
initiated
with the flick of a digit . . .
safety disengaged
final contact
between finger
and metal crescent

Projectile away
cartridge spent,
bullet flying
One more enemy of the state
left dead or dying.

First Rule of Correction

"Whack"
resonated the sound
of the wooden rule
hard, coming down
Breaking the silence
that hung in the air
like a mist
of sullen despair

Within a second
a collective gasp
raced audibly
through the room,
Another hand
had met its doom

Somewhere
in our austere chamber
decorated white
Another mate
had now, seen the light

No one moved
to say the least
For all had heard
the bellowing beast

Of all who heard
not one said, a single word
but all together
a mouthing choir
managed to whisper,
"yes, Sister"

"Silence is Golden
and I Want Some Gold!"
She shrieked out loud
as she stalked
and strutted
to the front of the crowd

No need to look
nor even to glance
no one dared peer
at the great, black and white bear

So familiar the sulk
of this habited hulk
All knew her sneer
permanently affixed there

One quickly learned
the fear and the dread
of daily confinement with she,
who seemed to have eyes

in the back of her head

Surely custom made
this flattened and measured
twelve inch blade
Perfect for punishing
each little bugger
Chip off the old block
from a Louisville slugger

Having experienced the trauma
of her unbridled wrath
which was channeled into
that appendage of ash
Wincing back
a single tear,
dripping to the page
like a drop of rain
Wondering whose hand
was now newly bludgeoned
Red with whelps
and searing pain

Recalling vividly
what little fun
was found at God's school
with the Sisterhood of Nuns
When I, was in grade one.

Food for Thought

How far away, are two
are we?

How much more time
'til we are to meet?

How long,
will it be

before we two
are both set free?

Fourteen generations,
Fourteen
and Fourteen more?

When will you rest
on that velvet floor?

Are we two destined
to be together

or will our experience
coexist never?

Awaiting your death
Awaiting my birth
Awaiting our introduction
In mother earth

How long before
we are both fed
You, God's fulfillment
You, my daily bread

For you are made man
Fated to die and decay
And I am made worm
Fated to hasten
your wasting away.

For The

For the drunk
it's his barstool
at his favorite place

For the super model
it's 'the look'
upon the face

For the sports fan
it's Sunday afternoon

For the musician
it's all
in the tune

For the depressed
it's in the confines
of a room

For the sycophant
it's in the glory
or the doom

For each and every one
it's different
Whether explore, expose
explode or exploit
Each has their own way
to fill the void

The emptiness of heart
A sense of despair
Avoiding the mirror's eyes
The ones that stare

For those in the mirror
know the truth,
and the truth is always
one hundred proof

When truth fills the void
as a hand in a glove
then in tandem lives
compassion and love

A heart with these three
is always triumphant
no matter the case
or what it may be

How does one acquire
said precious jewels?

Of the book, inquire
and use daily
it's tools

Start prior to death,
as close as possible to birth
The title of this Holy Grail?
Basic Instructions Before Leaving Earth.

Friends and Lovers

It started as friendship
It started
It started
It started
Well

You had what I wanted
I had what you needed
It started
It started
It started
Going well
It started

I cheated
You cried
I repeated
You lied
It started
It started
Not going so well
It started
It started

I repented
You relented
Damage done
On the run
It started
To unravel
It started
It started
It started

No more friendship
No more lovers
No more fun
beneath the covers
No more desire
even to try
It started
It started
It started
It started to die.

Gifts

I never bring you
baubles, bangles,
bright shiny things

No Pearls
No Opals
No Diamond rings

You never ask
argue,
fuss
nag or complain
When you don't receive
Silver
Gold
or Platinum chains

The gifts I have
For you my dear
Are in the words
You read and hear

How can I express
my undying love?

For you,
It is
just below Him
but for all other things
so far above

We are told
succinctly and bold
"Don't lay up your treasures
in silver and gold"

Put not one ounce
of value
Not one ounce
of trust
In those that are destined
for decay and rust

For you my love
eternally,
The gifts I bring
The gifts I give
Are in my poems
of and for you
That you and your soul
may have and enjoy
each heart felt word
for as long as you live.

He Whom He Sent

It's finally come
we did wait and wait
Hell's half fury
unleashed at the gate
What now to do?
Wonder and Watch?
Or become involved
beyond the couch?

Who is right?
Which can be wrong?
Only God knows
as He sits on His throne
King of all kings, Lord of all lords
At God's right hand
does He sit
God's own Son
'Son of Man'

Savior
Redeemer
Flesh of the One

Come to serve
the worst of us
that we might live
in His trust,
in His love
in His light
Through His Son
Through His own

He Whom He Sent
will carry me home.

Hiding From Ourselves

It seems obvious
after much ado
why so many women
now have silicone breasts
and god awful tattoos

They want us to concentrate
our staring gaze
anywhere,
except on their face
To insure that we
will never see
their hidden
insecurities

For men
it's easier
to deceive,
for natural born liars,
are we

With machismo
and material props
aiding to project

multi-layered
peacock facades
do we men erect

In this way
to an extreme
do men try and try
To insure
that we won't be,
looked in the eye.

Idols

The idols to which we bow and pay homage
spit on us and our insecurities.
They are created by us
that we might recognize something greater
than we
And the farthest we gaze
is to ourselves as their creators.

It may be one thing to create,
quite another to bestow blessings.
Playing at God does not equate to being God
any more than the ego to create,
bears blessings.

What greater self-duplicity
than to be the creators of our own idols
to which we then bow down?

Our identity crisis
cries out
for understanding and recognition.
Cries out
to all and any who would listen
with deaf ears,
as if to hear.
We cry and wonder

"How can I be so full of void?"
With passion we trade our blood, sweat and
tears
for the things of this world
While giving little. . . or worse,
"lukewarm" commitment
to the essence of life -
a personal spiritual relationship with God.

For the Spiritual Christian
everything needed, all facets in place
It is the choice of our heart
that determines our mask,
our cover,
our face.

Our actions; the seeds,
each new day do we sow
We always get
what we really want
That is for each
of us to know

Be it cash
or sacred cow
The questions are
to where, and to whom
will we bow?

Infidelity

Looking for my place now
at both rising and setting sun
How to fill the endless hours
now that you have gone

Like the slow beat
of the deep bass drum
everyone knew of your secret
everyone that is, lest one

What didn't you show
Why didn't I know
How far you would go
to make your point

You turned your back
on what once was us
Grasping all you could
of infatuation's salivating lust

Owner of two faces,
droll and carefree one
I kept no stride or pace,
with you on the run

You went from three to zero
looked like a million bucks
All smiles, new life, new friends,
no need now for blessing or luck

Stepping off the pages of Cosmo magazine
each and every glance in the mirror
an opportunity to make the scene
Looking back
a new you,
"Look at me now
I'm no longer blue"

I staggered
I fell
I felt like hell
Never knowing why,
I retreated
into my shell

Shorn of your mane
A new last name
From innocence to shame
The price of the game
You soon learned
as do we all
The damage done
from fidelity's fall

You soon learned
what you chose to do,
The impact it has…when it's done to you.

Living with Insecurities

Old doubts
Denials
and my double standard
Distrust of all the excuses I pander
Need for control
Wrath of my sting
These are a few of my favorite things

Fear of and loathing
your independence
Scary thoughts that last,
lovers
close friends
a special acquaintance
Figments from your past
Afraid of any, and all new arrivals
each and every
threatens my survival

When your phone rings
there's no answer
Where in the world
can you be?
Don't you know,
Don't you realize,
I'm all alone

with me

Corporate names
Logos, recognizable symbols
Each piece of clothing I own
has upon it at least
one branded identity
Printed,
patched or sown

Tattoos, piercings
permanent markings
cover and adorn my skin
Fitting to a proverbial 'T'
each pleads and screams
"Please, NOTICE ME !"

When your phone rings
there's no answer
Where in the world
can you be?
Don't you know,
Don't you realize,
I'm all alone
with me

Standing at the center of attention
of your world and mine

All is as,
it should be,
Its my way,
and all is fine

You call me inconsiderate
a fault finder
'poor me' attitude
But I have my own business cards
with inflated resume platitudes

Self inflicted paranoia
On my insistence you wear my ring
Fears and jealousy
Poutings and pleadings
Conflicts between us,
These are a few of my
favorite things

When your phone rings
there's no answer
Where in the world
can you be?
Don't you know,
Don't you realize,
I'm all alone
with me

I accuse you
my mind's remembrance
of all your liaisons past
Obsessed with your potential loss
Waiting for your double cross
With my fist I sent you reeling
But, you know
"I don't want to hurt your feelings"

In a guise
of trying to please,
by controlling your wants
your time
your needs
I say "I love you"
but we both know
the three little words
for which I pine,
are; I,
me,
and mine

Any criticism from outside
is, of course
a personal affront
Should you agree
with them just once

It is you
I shall have to shunt

Yes
I check up
and I follow,
yes
that's what I do
I can't help
that I'm always
chasing
and stalking you
Always knowing
Always thinking
you're in a sexual fling
"How long?" You ask
"From the beginning" I say
These are a few of my favorite things

When your phone rings
there's no answer
Where in the world
can you be?
Don't you know,
Don't you realize,
I'm all alone
with me

Someday, perhaps
I'll just say 'No'
but for now
I can't let you go
If you leave
finally breaking free
your new replacement will do
For I will find
yet another,
even more desperate than you

Yes, you'll be gone
free at last
that much may be true
but I'll still know
and yes, even then
I'll still spy on you too

When your phone rings
there's no answer
Where in the world
can you be?
Don't you know,
Don't you realize,
I'm all alone,
with me…

Lost

The world labeled me wild,
But you knew me lost
Sin invited me in,
Only you knew the cost

Season by season
I stumbled and fell,
Only you knew
I was headed for hell

Unable to scrape together
The dollars for bail,
The old judge just smiled
And sent me to jail
The next time we met
There were no tears,
The old judge just smiled
and said, "99 years."

I sit in my cell
And stare at the sink
All alone now
With more time to think

No friends to joke with
Party or drink

I sit in my cell
And stare at the sink

Alone and forgotten
Rotting away
Chalk on the wall
One slash for each day

What would I give
To do it again
What would I give
To be in your pen

To be one of your sheep
Instead of a goat
To hear your voice
My final hope
To hear your voice
To know your word
To follow your will
Finally,
free as a bird

A free bird still caged
Age after age
Trimmed and clipped wings
No longer enraged

Day after day
One step closer to death
No longer caged
Now, finally at rest
No longer alone
Having passed through your cross
Now flying with you Lord,
No longer lost.

Madonna Reincarnate

She arrives
one last time
Her last chance
to discover
Death's reason,
Life's rhyme

Final visit to each
New home to make
One lasting memory
From each to take

An image to hold
one for each so bold
to be held dear,
close and near
Until perhaps
once more to be known
the existence of each child's spirit
now to have grown

Old life behind her
New life ahead
The morning
she wakes
unconscious in bed

To meet
once again
by design
by luck,
or by chances wild?
Who will be parent?
Which will be child?

Maui Holiday

Sitting patiently
at Kahului airport
waiting,
on my next fare
Who it will be this time
another mainland stud
or a lady,
with flaxen hair?

Not really sure
which I enjoy more
Their colorful stories
or watching the masses
flow through the door

Suitcases and bags
grasped tightly in hand
Families search desperately
for their rental car van

Five hours or more
in the belly of the bird
Wonder what 'tales of the islands'
they've heard

Seven days from now
they'll be sunburned and tired
From a week's vacation
of mayhem and madness
All with new exploits
of tropical gladness

golf and tennis, snorkeling galore
hiking, biking, bus and copter tour
how many activities can we squeeze
into one day
well after all,
we did come to play

By the pool
or on the beach
drinks with umbrellas
within arm's reach

It's been said there's a hundred-and-one
things to do
and that's just the first week
if you are new

golf and tennis, snorkeling galore
hiking, biking, bus and copter tour
how many activities can we squeeze
into one day
hour upon hour,
in the sun's burning rays

Should we stop and get snacks
from Mana,,
before we start
the road to Hana

Tee off at Kapalua
Kaanapali
Wailea
After all,
we did drag these golf clubs
all the way-a

golf and tennis, snorkeling galore
hiking, biking, bus and copter tour
how many activities can we squeeze
into one day
this paradise calls to me,
"come run away"

Each night on Front Street
things really rock
all the way from Longhi's
down to the dock
Eating, drinking, dancing
and all in between,
make sure you're here
for at least one Halloween

golf and tennis, snorkeling galore
hiking, biking, bus and copter tour
how many activities can we squeeze
into one day
just one more week,
"please can't we stay"?

Sunrise at Haleakala,
or maybe sunset
either,
as long as we don't go to bed
Makawao cowboys
Honolua Bay wave riders
Ho'okipa windsurfers
and Molokini deep divers

golf and tennis, snorkeling galore
hiking, biking, bus and copter tour
how many activities can we squeeze
into one day,
hope our first day back home
is one with pay!

(Kahului [pronounced, Ka Hoo Loo Ee], Maui's
commercial community where the Maui airport is
located)
(Mana [pronounced, Ma Na], a health food store in
Paia [pronounced, Pie Ee Ah], Maui's 'Old
Plantation' community)
(Hana [pronounced, Ha Na], Maui's famous east side
community)
(Kapalua [pronounced, Ka Pa Loo Ah], Maui's upper
west side resort community)
(Kaanapali [pronounced, Ka On Ah Polly], Maui's
west side resort community)
(Wailea [pronounced, Why Lay Ah], Maui's south
side resort community)
(Haleakala [pronounced, Ha Lee Ah Ka La], Maui's
east side volcano mountain)
(Makawao [pronounced, Ma Ka Wow], Maui's
'upcountry' community, home to Maui's cowboys
and ranches)
(Honolua Bay [pronounced, Ho No Loo Ah], a bay
on Maui's upper west side famous for surfing)
(Ho okipa [pronounced, Ho O Keep Ah], beach on
the North Shore home of ld windsurfing
championships)
(Molokini [pronounced, Mo La Keen Ee], an atoll off
Maui famous for snorkeling and diving

Morning's Love

Dreaming of you
I awake to your presence
Each morning is almost
Like being in heaven

Your being,
Next to mine
Our souls,
Intertwined

Soft words whispered
The night before
To be with you
Forever more

Forever more
And one more day
Our spirits together
That we may stay,
Entwined
Ensconced
Entangled and bound,
In love
In lust
Infatuation still found

Found here
in this time
and in this place
Found there
after our time
in this human race

Our dreams fulfilled
in each other's arms
Each morning we wake,
another new day
together to face.

Name

I called your name

You heard
but would not listen
I wanted you christened

You, too busy chasing fame.

I spoke to you quietly

You heard
but would not heed
I offered to lead

You, turned away silently.

I came,
Again
and again
You wished only
to sin,
and sin

You, turning
this way and that

Me, refusing to give up
leaving you flat

Remain a captive
and follow your lust
or come,
join the three of us

What will it take,
for you to see

All I want,
is to set you free

So stand alone,
or become one with we three

For I have a plan
for each to hear
I have a path
for those who draw near
Open your mind
see what is clear
Know there is nothing
more to fear.

Your heart always knows the truth
Your heart never needs more proof

For you, for them,
it's all the same
I treat all alike

I simply, called your name.

Night and Day

Southwestern Sol dips
behind mountain's forested rim
Sangria De Christo sunset
the air begins to thin

Coalescing crimsons
start to take shape
Before on-looking eyes
descends twilight's
fuchsia drape

Light giving way to darkness
arriving from the east
Day's blazon heat
fades and slips, into sleep

One by one
each star's rebirth
takes place in heaven
above this earth

Twinkling,
pin points of light
like holes
in the black of night
Piercing
the canopy dark
as if pricked, by ethereal darts

Dark chasing light
day follows night,
or is it
the other way around?
Which be first
and by which
are we bound?

Never,
to fully comprehend
For as we are told,
it is light that bends.

Noetic Conversation
[Mind Talk (*with God*)]

me
me
me
me
me
me,
You

(Yes)

my needs
my wants
my true desires

(I Know)

Like blue flames
of red raging fires

(You)

Love
Understanding
Compassion
Forgiveness; All free

(Learn)

Hidden behind veils of being one
other than me

(My Will)

To be at rest

(My Ways)

From my ways
From my work

(My Words)

From my words
From the daily struggles

(My Son)

With which I flirt

(All Given)

Please, please
Give me rest

(For You)

From all this pain
From all this hurt

Eternally.
(Eternally).

Now and Then

The years. . .
Where have they gone?
Last mustache. . .
dark, long and strong
New attempt. . . .
gray, thick and worn,
Fifteen years passed

Memories. . .
just a few
Thoughts. . .
one or two,
of you
Wondering. . .
if you knew,
What I felt

Wanting to please
at every twist and turn
Having your way
your every urge and yearn
Each weekend
little did I learn,
About you

Conditioned love. . .
maybe more than friends
Reality. . .
even at the end
Pain and pleasure. . .
passion too
A caged bird
you finally gave a clue
It was over
at least it was, for you,
Goodbye

Six months. . .
that's all it took
Six months. . .
I recognized that look
Six months. . .
for you
to shake loose
Inhibition
Guilt
and Shame
About playing
your needed, hidden game

Should have told me. . .
At the start
At hello
Then we both. . .
both would have known
No inhibitions
No guilt
No shame
What we wanted. . .
all the time
was the same

Conditioned love. . .
kept us in the dark
Conditioned love. . .
kept us both apart
Apart in truth
From what we wanted
just to share
Apart, alone
truth no longer
be laid bare

Conditioned love. . .
Relationship
disrepair
Each alone. . .
final self-despair,
It's over

All along. . .
we always knew
All along. . .
Nothing left to do
Go on alone
Once again
Once again that's true
No need to feel
lonely
black or blue,
All alone

Separate ways
Separate paths
Alone again
No more laughter
No more wrath

It was fun
It was good. . .
For me
For you,
No future.

Number Please

Within this state of confusion
and the general state of the world
It's fairly obvious
for every boy,
and for every girl
Soon the rules will change,
in today's name game
and sooner than later
not one,
will ever be named the same

A number
should suffice
Because they're all
distinctively nice,
no duplicates
mix ups
juniors
or whatever
Just a simple ID
to be used forever

We currently use numbers
and their combinations
for every conceivable transaction
across ours,
and every nation

With this in mind
I would like to say
from this point forward
from this day on
no longer will I
be known as John,
For business
personal
or recreational fun
From now on please address me as;
97436421.

O Lord

The nearer I draw to you O Lord
The closer I long to be
The more of you, You show me O Lord
The more I desire to see.

On Display

Breasts
and bellies show
Burnt to bronze
skin aglow
Postage stamp
once unfolded
covers nipple
and areola

Impressions
to be made,
Notoriety's name
as well
Life's fast lane
to be traveled
Party Party
What the hell

Journey-woman plumber?
Plumber in training?
Off her hips
denim is draining
At the bottom
of a back
cheeks peek,
top of a crack

Star,
soon to be
Yes,
"It's all about me"
Move over Kidmans,
Anistons,
or whoever
The world's gift now here
burning out, yes
leaving, never

Short shorts?
Shorter,
No, shorter still
Leave nothing to imagination
subtle desires
comely will

Look please
at my body
my teats, my ass
Not to my soul
behind these eyes
where the frightened child
inside,
still cries

Six-pack abs
you too can get
Six hours a day
in the gym
no sweat

Biceps, triceps,
Quads
Man of steel
Ready for video
or perhaps
reel to reel

Impressions
to be made,
Notoriety's name
as well
Life's fast lane
to be traveled
Party Hardy
What the hell

Journeyman mechanic?
Soon to be grease wrencher
Of all trades jack
Only
the monkey,
is still on his back

Star,
soon to be
Yes,
"It's all about me"
Move over Cruises,
Pitts,
or whoever
The world's gift now here
burning out, yes
leaving, never

Admire my body
my bravado, imitative style
With ego's shovel
passive and unimaginative rhetoric
do I pile

Look please
at my aura
my pose, my allure
Not to my soul
behind these eyes
where the frightened child
inside,
still hides.

Once Upon A Walk

Stick
and Bone
and Leaf
and Rock
these four I found
while on my walk

Stick once lived and now is dead
Bone having come from some skeletal head
Leaf has turned from green to reddish gold
all part of the process of growing old

and Rock, what of you
from whence have you come
from what part
of the original load
were you taken
to be part of this road

you, small Rock with your family and
friends
all joined together here, here at the end
end of the lane, end of the street
without you mighty Rock
no route is complete

it is you mighty Rock who forms
the foundation,
the path and the way,
for a wandering nation

mighty Rock, it is upon your back
that Stick
and Bone
and Leaf
do alight
during the day
and during the night

each at the end of their personal race
looking to you for a loving embrace
for it is only upon you mighty Rock
from your passionate grace,
that Stick
and Bone
and Leaf
find their final resting place.

One Luxury

She enters
replete with
homeless gear
Living off
and on
the street
now nearly a year

Prior to bedding
and after her toilet
she pauses,
body oil to fetch

A single
anointing gesture,
borrowed luxury
once taken,
never to be taken
from her.

Paradise Found

We met at a bar
on the sands of Waikiki
Her last night in town
drinking Mai Tai
and Long Island Ice Tea

She and a friend
decided to shoot the moon
Get loose, get crazy,
they surveyed the room

Our eyes met,
not fatal attraction
but both of us knew
we were up for some action

Small talk
A couple of jokes
One more round
Outside for a toke

Leaving her friend
and my brother behind
We lay on the sand
and started to grind

Her pelvis in motion
legs interlocked
without adieu
I was hard as a rock

Hands massaging
the small of her back
The smell of her skin
her scent on attack

Stopping a moment
figures on the lanai
She let out a laugh
I thought was a cry

She standing over me
us both now erect
she stripped off her clothes
I said, "What the heck"

We ran naked to the water's edge
as her friend and my brother
looked over the rail
of the patio's ledge

She said "come with me baby"
and sprinted aloft
Breasts bouncing,
hair flowing
bronzed skin,
tan lines showing

Hitting cold water
I went flaccid
and soft
Standing in ocean up to her nipples
arms round my neck
lips to mine
She whispered,, "let's keep this simple"
I moaned,
"That's fine"

Hand in hand
we ran up the beach
a secluded and private
spot did we reach

Relaxing supine
night's sand on my spine
both knew we were in
for one hell of a time

Lips to lips
tongue on the tip
Sixty eight plus one
we both started to lick

Nibble the hood
darting below
sweet musk liquid
started to flow
Thumb and finger
both buried deep
sheath of tissue
wet in between

Dreamily wanting
never to stop
Next thing I knew
she was mounted on top

Large firm breasts
cupped in my hands
Hardened engorged member
wrapped tight by her glands

Up
and
down,
she slowly rode
I fought back the urge
to release all my load

As we thrust rapidly
against one another
squatted above me
she impaled herself
like no other

Both adrift
in our lands of nether
final explosion
we came together

Exhausted and spent
we lay entangled
Two lifeless forms,
racked and mangled

Eye to eye
and breath to breath
smiling broadly she said,
"I have a plane to catch".

(Waikiki [pronounced Why Key Key],
the famous beach area of Honolulu
[pronounced Ho No Loo Loo] on the island
of Oahu [pronounced O Ah Oo])
(Lanai [pronounced La Nye], a porch or
patio)

Passion Soliloquy

Four comments from His lips
over less than one day's span
Tell of His conquest
over sin and death
showing us the way,
This Son of Man

His humanity spark
momentarily,
Asking if He must "take this cup"
cup of our responsibility,
Next thought
the Father's will
of His love
there is enough

Hanging up
looking down
Tilted heads skyward
eyes from the ground
"Forgive them Father,
they know not what they do"
Believing they silence me
Believing they follow you

This world's sin
is truly great
and of His being
did it satiate
Sin bearing down
a burden too great to carry
yet not one minute
did He tarry

As heavy a ransom
as there could be
"Why my God oh why
have you forsaken me?"
Not forsaken
now I see
though you've turned away

Clearly now
of this world's sin
not even a trace
shall transgress your face

For all who follow
and believe in me
there is eternal life
And to the faithful
of my words

certainly they will win it
Sins of all
now taken on
purpose and role fulfilled,
Finally, with one last breath,
"It is finished".

Right Now

Right Now,
Right at this very moment
Somewhere in the world
Somewhere on the planet
Someone is,
strolling on a country lane
attending to a chronic pain
receiving a traffic ticket
chasing dinner through a thicket
blowing their stuffy nose
tickling a baby's toes
saying, 'I don't know'
refusing to grow
making mad passionate love
in a park
feeding a dove
inventing a new device
cheating on a cheating wife
quarreling and throwing fists
slicing a pair of wrists
someone is buying
someone is selling
someone is yelling
someone is felling
a tree

one is paying a fee
another is breaking a knee
someone is taking a pea
on a fork
having a snort
filing a legal tort
coming into port
building a cardboard fort
making a caustic retort
just about to abort
passing gas as a smelly fart
throwing a steel tipped dart
going on a summer lark
in a play reciting the line
'Hark'
making a large dog bark
standing stark
naked
a child is saying 'I hate you'
a child is saying 'I love you'
a lady has the flu
a man has lost his shoe
a teenager is turning blue
a crying mother says 'I wish I knew'
a boy really is named Sue
(No not really)
but someone somewhere is peeling

someone else is pealing
and a third is pealing out in a car
burning rubber
one is having supper
another lunch
yet another breakfast
and yet another, brunch
a young woman feels all alone
one is on the phone
someone has just sown
a seed
pulled a weed
been in need
tossing feed
wetting a reed
for a wind instrument
having a fit
suckling a teat
tonguing a clit
as a woman asks
'where are all the good men'?
the Marines say
they have 'a few good men'
a prayer ends with amen
somewhere a rooster chases a hen
a man has just broken his pen
a bank is ready to lend

a shirt is on the mend
a woman is having to fend
off an attacker
someone is playing a hunch
an uncle is throwing a punch
an aunt is feeling the crunch
a toothless man is trying to munch
his snack
before he has his heart attack
someone is coming back
someone is leaving
someone is going home
someone is reading a poem

about
Right Now.

Shelby Bright Eyes

My old dog and I
take a walk everyday
To the mailbox and back
the two of us stray

Come rain or shine
the two of us go
Sort of hand in paw,
don't you know

She hobbles down hill
I hobble up
Seems like just yesterday
we were both pups

Having a pet
is a glorious thing
As we look each other in the eye
I could swear both our hearts sing

That dog's a protector
whether I see her or not
No one comes near our property
without getting caught

Now she's too old to bite
and too old to fight
And she would never, ever attack
To tell the truth
most of the time
she's a little laid back

But I'll guarantee
all times day or night
If she senses alarm
or that something's not right
She'll sure as hell bark
and raise such a clatter
I'll know a stranger is here
and that's all that matters

I love that old dog
and I know she loves me
And together we make
a pretty good we

It's been said that a dog
is man's best friend
and that they'll be faithful
right up to the end
Having owned quite a few
I tend to agree

Dogs must have been put here
for you, and for me

All part of a plan
A plan of His,
for we all know
what DOG,
spelled backward is.

Sirens Call

Your voices in the distance call
Melodically to the ears of men
From across the skies and universe of light
Gaining our attention
Piercing the dark of night

What is it, you Sirens sing?
Voices scaling all musical notes
Up and down,
songs revealing your host
Do we hear,
did we ever
As you give your vocal toast
to the love and truth of His angels wings

A taste of love understood
from where you stand
All vocal members
A universal band
Without your perfect pitch
would we be led astray
Forever,
and for one more day

You call to us
your voices so ripe
Reverberating aloud
through the silent night
Refusing to heed
your call
your song
your whisper
your breath,
Now singing no more
all voices at rest.

Sixty Minutes

One hour to go
if it would only
go slow,
waiting,
while knowing
there is no control,
no relief
waiting now
upon the thief

Thief in the night
thief of life
nemesis of the living
always taking,
never giving

Last breath
Last thought
Last vision
Last words,
what will they be?

The final realization
a plea for reconstitution
an act of reinstatement
perhaps reincarnation,
A cry for forgiveness

To look eye to eye
with the one,
the Christ,
or
to face the heat
to sleep and wait,
which
is the slated fate

Minutes left
only a few
the choice,
eternity
to win or lose.

State of Being

Unconditional love
is impossible for humans
From our first moment of existence
From our first breath
We live in a conditioned state of being

The closest we come
to experiencing God
is to serve the needs of others

Serving is never exclusively
ecumenical
parochial
evangelical
or dogmatic
It is seeing a need
and filling it compassionately
Recognizing a wrong
and righting it truthfully
Having love and sharing it honestly

Serving is love in action.

Teed Off

Hit me again,
harder

Go ahead
hit me,
hit me again
harder than you did the last time

I welcome your assault
I've come to learn
and expect it from you

You can hit me
with the club
if you want
I can take it

I'll take all
you can dish out
Even though I have
a cut or two
please don't discard me

My dimples
are intact for you
My smile
as white as ever
Wash the dirt off
from your abuse
and I will remain
yours still

My only desire
is to be the one
you reach for
each time
you tee up to drive
May I always be
your favorite
golf ball.

The Nature of Things

The leaves sing your praises Lord
as winds from your breath
rustle limbs and branches,
whispering to us
of life and death

Your tears
rain down upon us
the more we stray
and the farther we drift
from your loving way

The stars above us
in the day's night sky
are as seeds you have sown
with a wave of your hand
That we might see them
from each and every land

Nature in this world
speaks only of you
Since the beginning
that has been true

Of course all that changed
once man made his things
in his own name

The ones you made
still honor and bow
The ones man made
demand kowtow

You sent us a servant
to show us the way
The way back to you
with each new day

A simple plan really,
when each night is done
with each new day's rising,
acknowledge the Son.

Today

Living in the past
Anticipating the future
What am I going to do,
Today

Remembering glory days
Fearing the unknown ahead
How to make the transition between the two,
Today

Existence
Only in the present
Reality
This twenty-four hours,
Today

Experiencing events
Which envelope my senses
Active or passive response,
Today

Smiles, Tears
Love, Hate
Commitment, Indifference
Life, Death,
Today

Who was I?
Who will I be?
Who is it the world sees
when looking at me?
Who's face in the mirror
stares back at me?
Who am I?
Today.

Vacation in Spain

Let's get away
Let's go on holiday
Let's leave behind
The familiar day's grind

Let's get freedom's reprieve
And needed revitalment
From the work-a-day world
Of corpus confinement

Where can we go
To get away from life's pain
Let's travel to
the Costa del Sol,
In old southern Spain

Upon our arrival
Hotel room upon room
More confinement cubicles
To seal our doom

Little boxes
Green, brown and blue
More corpus cubicles
Just different hues
Stacked atop one on another
Space not available
Our privacy
Our senses
All assailable

From Attico A
On the fourteenth floor
The teeming of peoples
More upon more
Thinking, believing
They all 'have it made'
In vacation's concrete cells
of mortar and clay

How many of us work
And struggle in life
How dearly we pay
Husband, child and wife
For a week's reprieve
Or maybe for two

Away from confinement
The kind we all knew
Each knowing quite well
Forty-eight to fifty weeks
of working hell

The sun comes up
Blazen' heat doth arrive
A new day's furnace lit
'oer the Med's eastern sky

En Los Boliches
Soon will they stream
Attempts to escape
Concrete's heat
Concrete's steam

Day's heat won't relent
Beach visitors,
Exhausted and spent
At day's end, all return
Sporting epidermal souvenirs
Bright scarlet sunburns

Back into cubicles
Ten by twelve
Do they delve
One more day's vacation
More memories do they shelve

Thousands upon tens
Visitors, tourists
Passers through,
Dream vacations
in corpus cubicles,
Green, brown and blue.

Veils

The dryness masked in green
Shadows deceiving a moisture hidden
No, a false sense
The coming of Autumn
The onslaught of Winter
Truth veiled in reality before our very eyes.

The forests speak to us
while our cities remain silent
The trees and shrubs
give back their life force
While man's stone edifices
and marble markers
Tell only of short-lived grandeur.

Waves

The waves roll ever onward,
struggling against the push of the wind
and the pull of the current
persistent, to reach the shore.

To become one with the sand
to feel the substance of land,
next to the liquidness of their existence
is their goal and ambition.

To have but one moment
of blended bliss
before being forced to recede
back into ocean's abyss.

Often times they come crashing
part of a thunderous force
which carries them over
all obstacles on course.

Without the storming surge from afar
the waves are destined to wait their turn
their one opportunity to lap gently
against the earth
that forms their eternal floor

which has now crept up,
to become the shore.

Wet and dry convoluted band
separates two worlds,
one of endless water
the other endless land.

The waves ride the backs
of their brothers and sisters below
spurred on by the winds
called hither by the voices
of ancient mariners
and distant songs
of mythological sirens.

Great creatures of both man and nature
disrupt and tear through them,
but in the wakes left behind
the waves simply return
to merge in their dance and union
ever onward, to the shore.

The day's heat evaporates
and claims their numbers
just as the rains replenish their losses,
and still their march continues
ever onward, to the shore.

Too much and we are doomed
Not enough and life perishes
And still the waves reach out
traveling mile after mile
to feel the touch of land
and be one with the shore.

Wedding Bell Blues

She leads
He follows
She buys
He sighs
He tugs
She shrugs
He tells her not to buy
Again,
She wonders why

When was the day
and How,
did it get this way
Had she only realized
Before,
her wedding day

Why hadn't she listened
Why hadn't she known
what lay dormant
what lay waiting
in her soon to be
(un)happy home

the struggles
the strife
the arguments
the fights
over this
over that
over the kids
over the cat,
over money,
too much spent
not enough coming in
so much wasted,
for both
a no win

Had they only known
in those 'good old days'
how much toil
how much trouble
was headed their way

They were in love
they told themselves so
and anyone else
who wanted to know

Whether love
or lust
or infatuation
if only they'd heard
those whispered words,
"Go slow"

High school over
end of the trail
next step together
would be a clear sail

In a hurry
without a worry
"That"
would never
happen to them,
as it had,
to all of their friends

Then came the house
kids
dog
and the cat
With a seven year itch
he became a rat,

for both,
the feeling was 'trapped'

Time passing
stuck in the mire
matrimonial struggles
making each of them tired,
tired of this
sick of that
tired of each other
sick of it all,
him at the bar
her at the mall

Going,
their own separate ways
Two peas in a pod
Alone together now
in name and facade

Had they only waited
through their teens
and their twenties
they would have found
time aplenty

Time to grow
Time to know
Themselves, each other
More friends
Other lovers

Still, fate may have found them
just once more
in each other's arms
at each other's door

Life's stage set differently,
more mature
more alive
more demure
more aware
more to share
more to care,
more soul
to bear

Love's song lost
No retrievable cost
The die is cast
and in the end
their story to be told
at long last

but for now,
mutual resistance
and total indifference.

Other books by Branch Isole

Seeds of Mana'o © Thoughts, Ideas &
Opinions in Poetic Prose
ISBN 0-9747692-1-5

Messages in a Bottle © Inspirations in
Poetic Prose   ISBN 0-9747692-9-0

Saccharin and Plastic Band Aids ©
Comments in Poetic Prose
ISBN 0-9747692-8-2

Power of Praise © The Poetry of Spiritual
Christianity™   ISBN 0-9747692-7-4

God. . .i believe © Simple Steps on the Path
of Spiritual Christianity ™
ISBN 0-9747692-0-7

Even Christians Stumble and Fall ©
Musings of a Struggling Believer
ISBN 0-9747692-4-X

Crucibles © Refinement of the Neophyte
Christian   ISBN 0-9747692-3-1

To order, call toll free 1-866-410-4440

Printed in the United States
49074LVS00001B/28-75